Amazon Fire Stick 4k Max for Beginners

An Easy, and Illustrative Guide With Tips and Tricks on How to Master the Fire Stick 4K Max

Jessica Peters

© COPYRIGHT 2021 JESSICA PETERS - ALL RIGHTS RESERVED.

The content contained within this book may not be reproduced, duplicated or transmitted without direct written permission from the author or the publisher.

Under no circumstances will any blame or legal responsibility be held against the publisher, or author, for any damages, reparation, or monetary loss due to the information contained within this book. Either directly or indirectly.

Legal Notice:

This book is copyright protected. This book is only for personal use. You cannot amend, distribute, sell, use, quote or paraphrase any part, or the content within this book, without the consent of the author or publisher.

Disclaimer Notice:

Please note the information contained within this document is for educational and entertainment purposes only. All effort has been executed to present accurate, up to date, and reliable, complete information. No warranties of any kind are declared or implied. Readers acknowledge that the author is not engaging in the rendering of legal, financial, medical or professional advice. The content within this book has been derived from various sources. Please consult a licensed professional before attempting any techniques outlined in this book.

By reading this document, the reader agrees that under no circumstances is the author responsible for any losses, direct or indirect, which are incurred as a result of the use of the information contained within this document, including, but not limited to, — errors, omissions, or inaccuracies.

AMAZON FIRE STICK 4K MAX GUIDE

TABLE OF CONTENTS

INTRODUCTION 13

Interface 15

Remote 16

CHAPTER ONE 17

Setup 17

How to Manually Pair Your Remote 23

How to Use the Remote Control 25

Using the Remote 28

How to Use the Text Banner Feature 31

How to Restart Your Fire TV Stick 33

How to Find 4k Content 35

How to Use Alexa 38

How to Use the Alexa App 39

How to Connect Your Alexa Device to Fire TV...........41

Best Alexa Fire TV Commands....................................42

How to Use VPN on the Fire Stick/TV.............................44

Which VPN Should I go for? 45

How to install a VPN from the Amazon app store 48

How to Use a Mouse with the Fire TV Stick 52

How to update your VPN app 53

Troubleshooting...53

CHAPTER TWO 55

How to Install Apps 55

How to download apps from the Amazon app store **55**

How to Use the Search Function to Find and Download Apps 57

How to Download Apps to a Fire TV Stick Using the Amazon Website? 60

How to Enable Third-Party Apps in Settings on Fire Stick 62

How to side-load apps 64

How to Uninstall Apps 68

How to Delete All Apps via Factory Reset 73

How to Clear an App's Data 74

How to Update an App 76

How to Update Side-Loaded Apps? 77

How to Create an App Shortcut 79

How to use the Fire Stick Remote Shortcuts 81

AMAZON FIRE STICK 4K MAX GUIDE

How to Update My Fire Stick 84

How to Activate Sleep Mode 87

Best Settings for the Fire Stick 88

1. Manage Your Privacy Settings and Disable Data Monitoring 88

2. Change the Amazon App Store Settings. 92

3. Change App Notification Settings 96

4. Disable Video and Audio AutoPlay 98

CHAPTER THREE 100

How to Manually Enable Parental Control 100

How to Manage Parental Control settings 100

How to Enable Parental Controls 102

How to Change Parental Control PIN on Fire Stick? 103

How to Disable Focused Adverts..................................104

How to Turn Subtitle On/Off? 106

   Main Fire TV Setting..106

   Amazon Prime Video...108

   Netflix 108

   Disney+ 109

   YouTube..109

   Apple TV+...110

   HBO Max...110

   IMDB TV 110

   Sling TV 110

How to Use Netflix 111

   How to Sign Up for Netflix 111

How to Use YouTube 113

　　How to Sign Up for YouTube 114

　How to Use the Watch List? 115

　　How to Add Content to The Watch List? 116

　How to Use the X-Ray Feature? 117

CHAPTER FOUR 119

　How to Monitor Data Usage? 119

　　How to Check App Data Usage? 120

　　How to Set Data Cap Value? 121

　　Check App Data Usage by Apps 121

　How to Mirror Your Laptop to The Fire Stick? 122

　How to Mirror Your Smartphone to The Fire Stick? 126

　　How to activate the Mirroring feature on your Fire

TV? 126

How to Cast an Android Phone 128

How to Cast iOS Phones and Tablets to your Fire Stick
....130

Mirroring via Third-Party Apps in Android 132

How to Use 5ghz Network on your streaming stick 134

What Is 5GHz? 134

How to Switch Your Router to 5GHz 136

How to Pair Fire Stick with a Bluetooth Speaker? 138

How do I connect the Fire Stick to Bluetooth devices?
....138

CHAPTER FIVE 142

How to Use Your Phone as a Remote? 142

AMAZON FIRE STICK 4K MAX GUIDE

How to Set up the Fire Stick Remote App 142

How to Use the Fire TV Stick Remote App? 145

How to Create a Digital Phone Frame On the Fire TV?150

Creating a Photo Screensaver 150

How to customize photo slideshows?......................151

How to Configure the Volume and Power Controls? ..152

How to Install IMDB TV on Fire Stick............................154

CHAPTER SIX 156

Troubleshooting Issues 156

Can't connect to a Wi-Fi network 156

Fire TV logo is stuck on the screen..........................157

Fire Stick won't turn on..157

Apps crash or refuse to load 158

Fix Screen Mirroring Issues 159

Update Your Fire Stick...160

INTRODUCTION

The Amazon Fire TV Stick 4K Max is here, and it comes with a lot of new promising features and upgrades. This streaming stick is available on Amazon for £54.99, and it is 40% more powerful than the Fire TV Stick 4K.

For the first time, Amazon's fire stick supports Wi-Fi 6, allowing you to stream and game more smoothly and fluidly. Of course, to use this, you'll need a Wi-Fi router, preferably one that supports Wi-Fi 6.

With this streaming stick, you can enjoy faster app launches and a better cinematic experience. It also comes with an Alexa Voice Remote that allows you to search for and activate apps using your voice. With Alexa, you can control your smart home devices, get weather updates, watch videos in Picture-in-Picture mode, and much more. This streaming stick can also be used to stream sports and news.

Interface

Like the previous Fire TV Stick, the interface of this streaming stick is centered on Amazon's ecosystem. Sign up for Amazon Prime to gain full access to all the Fire Stick's features as well as personalized recommendations from Prime Video and Amazon-owned IMDb TV.

The newly updated Fire TV interface is more colorful than ever, and it has been redesigned with three tabs- The Home, Find, and Live tab. The Home tab displays all of your recommended apps and content, while the Find tab is used to locate content easily.

Note that you'll be getting a lot of sponsored ads and banners at the top of your Fire TV screen.

Remote

This Fire TV Stick remote features a blue Alexa button for interacting with Alexa, and it supports Alexa Voice. The remote is also designed with a select button in the middle, menu buttons, Back and Options buttons, TV power and volume buttons, and navigation buttons.

Unfortunately, Amazon has included branded app buttons to this remote, making lots of ads pop up on your TV screen. The buttons are dedicated to Prime Video (of course), Disney Plus, Netflix, and Amazon Music.

CHAPTER ONE

Setup

When you open your Fire Stick 4k Max box, you'll find:

- An Alexa remote

- The Fire TV Stick

- HDMI Extender

- Power Adapter

- Two Remote Batteries

- A USB cable and a

- Quick Start Guide

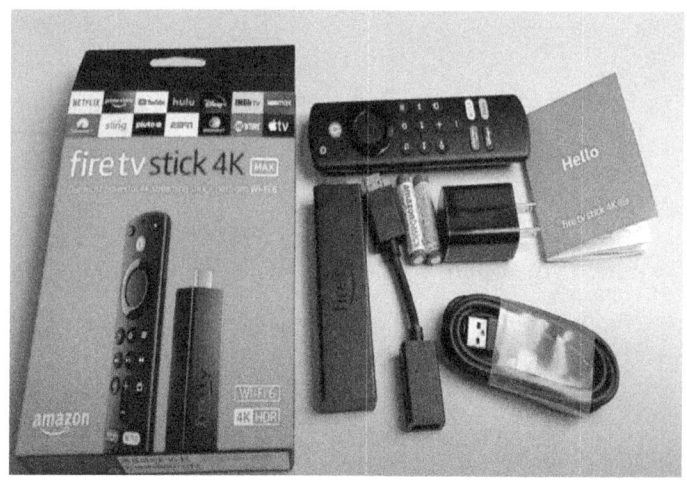

The USB cord and power adapter aren't required during the setup process, although they help to improve performance. Now, here's how to set up this device:

- Grab the HDMI extender and connect it to the Fire Stick
- Connect one end of the micro USB cable to the power adapter and the other end to the Fire Stick's power port. If your power adapter isn't

working, you can also plug in the USB cable to any open USB port on your TV.

- Note that you can use this streaming device on any compactable TV with an HDMI port, including smart TVs and non-smart TVs.
- Connect this streaming stick to your TV and connect the power adapter to a power outlet. Your connected cables should look like this:

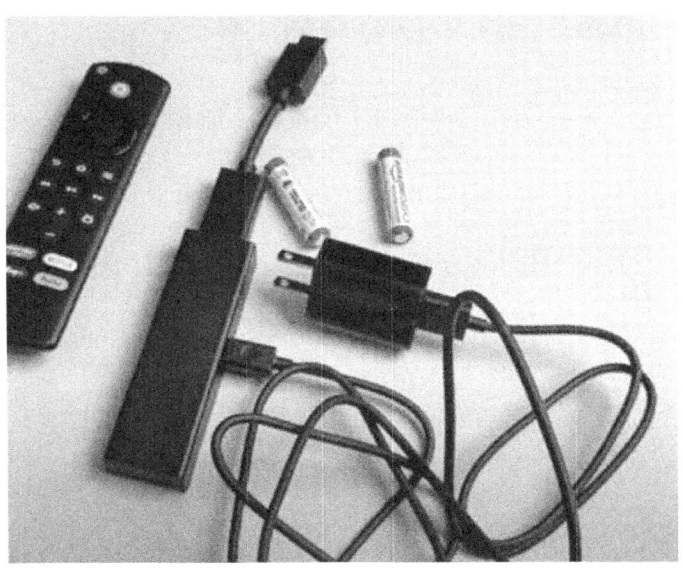

- Next, insert the batteries into your Fire Stick remote, turn on your TV, and find the correct HDMI port. It could be HDMI 1, HDMI 2, or HDMI 3. Your TV should automatically pair with the remote after inserting the batteries.

- If you have trouble with this step, hold the remote closer to your Fire TV Stick and then hold down the Home for 10 seconds. If nothing works, change your batteries, unplug the Fire TV Stick from the power supply, and then plug it back in after a few minutes.

- Press Play/Pause on your remote, select your preferred language and choose your preferred Wi-Fi network.

- Wait a moment while your TV installs the latest software, and then click on "Sign in to your amazon account" after the TV restarts.

- Next, head to the website at "amazon.com/code," sign in, and type in the activation code displayed on your TV screen.

- Click on Continue, select your preferred Parental Control settings, and then click Next on the volume check screen. Use your TV's remote to turn up the TV's volume.

- Point your Fire remote to your TV screen as instructed, test its volume buttons and then click Yes if they responded. That's it!
- Now click OK to go to the home screen.
- Next, sign up for "Amazon Kids+" and then click on Get started to walk through Amazon's app downloads on-boarding
- Next, select your preferred TV channel apps and services. Right-click to move to the next page/options
- Select your preferred service and click on Pay at the bottom to proceed
- Wait for the download to be completed and then click on "Got It" to proceed
- If you've set up Parental control, then enter your pin and select a user profile. You are good to go

AMAZON FIRE STICK 4K MAX GUIDE

How to Manually Pair Your Remote

If you couldn't pair your Fire remote during the setup process, here's how to do that manually:

- First, you have to download the Fire TV app and pair it to your smartphone.
- Turn on your Fire TV, insert your Voice Remote batteries, and move your remote close to your Fire TV.
- Unplug your Fire TV from its power source and plug it back in.
- Open the Fire TV app on your smartphone, and make sure the app has been paired to your Fire TV.
- Head to your Fire TV's settings, go to "Controllers & Bluetooth Devices," click on

"Amazon Fire TV Remotes," and select "Add New Remote."

- Select your new remote from the list and click on it to pair. That's it.

How to Use the Remote Control

This guide will acclimate you to the remote control functions of your Amazon Fire Stick 4K Max streaming device. First, let's look at the buttons on the remote

- Power Button: Controls both your TV and Fire Stick 4k Max
- LED Light: Illuminates when buttons are pushed
- A Microphone: For using voice commands
- Voice Control Button: For using voice commands
- Navigation Ring: Controls functionality, menus, guides, and more
- Select Button: To OK the desired command

- Back Button: Returns to previously viewed screens
- Home Button: Returns to the home screen
- Menu Button: This takes you directly to the Fire TV's menu
- Rewind Button: For rewinding a program
- Play/Pause Button: Starts and stops the program you are watching
- Fast Forward Button: Advances the program you are watching
- Volume Button: Controls the audio level on your TV
- Mute Button: Pauses sound

JESSICA PETERS

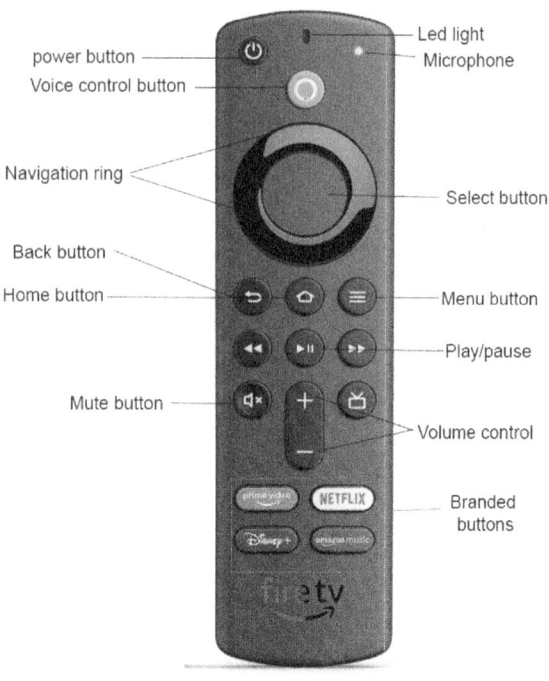

Using the Remote

Now, here's how to use your remote control easily

- First, click the Menu button☰ to get to the main menu and then use the Select button to access the Fire TV guide.

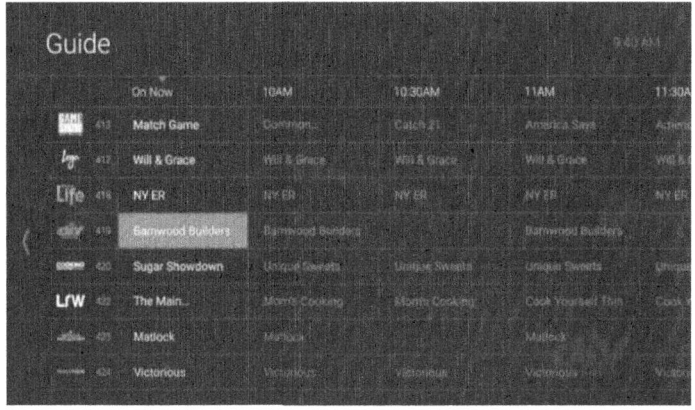

- Use the navigation ring to go up and down the channel listing

- Click the RIGHT button to see upcoming shows on a channel and LEFT to go back to the current show area

- Now click the select button on a show. This will reveal the options to Play, Record, or see Program Information. Click the SELECT button again to watch the program.

- If you want to use Fire TV's restart feature to start the show over from the beginning, simply click the SELECT button again.

- Use the PLUS (+) or MINUS (-) button to raise or lower your TV volume.

- Use the Fast-Forward button to jump ahead of the show.

- While watching a show, click up or down on the navigation ring to change channels without using the guide.

- To return to a previous show, click the back button to return to the main menu. While the word guide is highlighted, click the Down function on the navigation ring to see the last several channels you were watching.

- To return to the guide, click the back button twice and then click the select button. Click the Left button to access Fire TV's Replay function and filters.

How to Use the Text Banner Feature

Amazon has included a Text Banner feature for those with vision impairments. Once enabled, users can easily tell what section of the screen is selected.

- First, head to the Fire TV menu, go to Settings, and click on Accessibility.

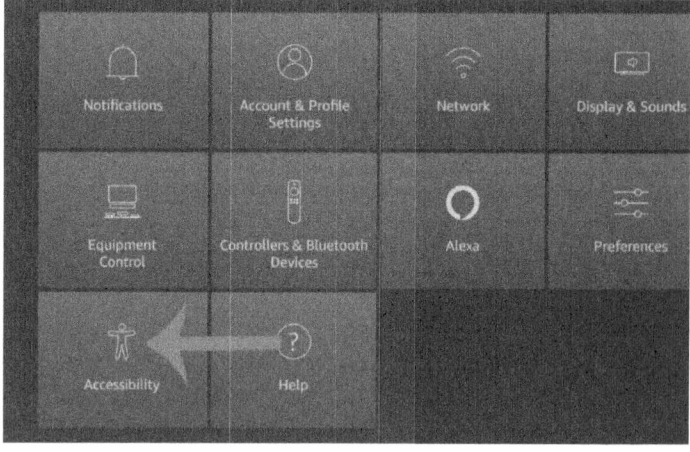

- Click on "Text Banner" and customize the settings the way you want them.

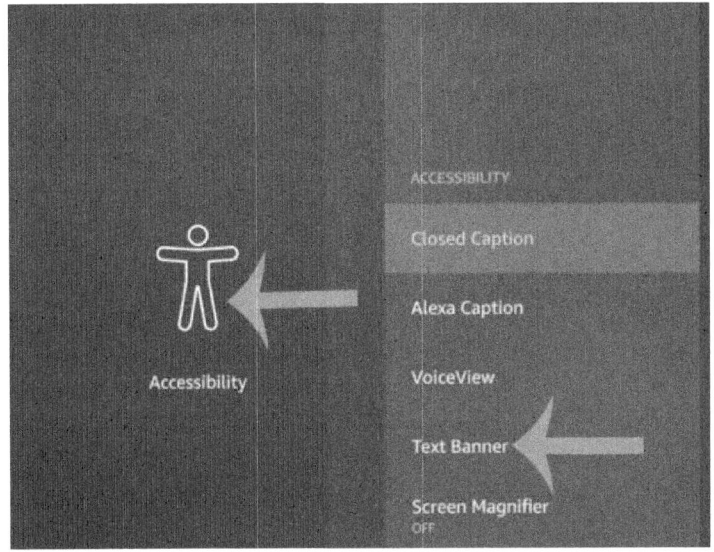

- Once you're done, the text banner will be displayed according to your settings.

How to Restart Your Fire TV Stick

If you want to restart your Fire Stick, here are two ways to do that

- Head to your Fire TV's settings, go to "My Fire TV" and click on the Restart option.

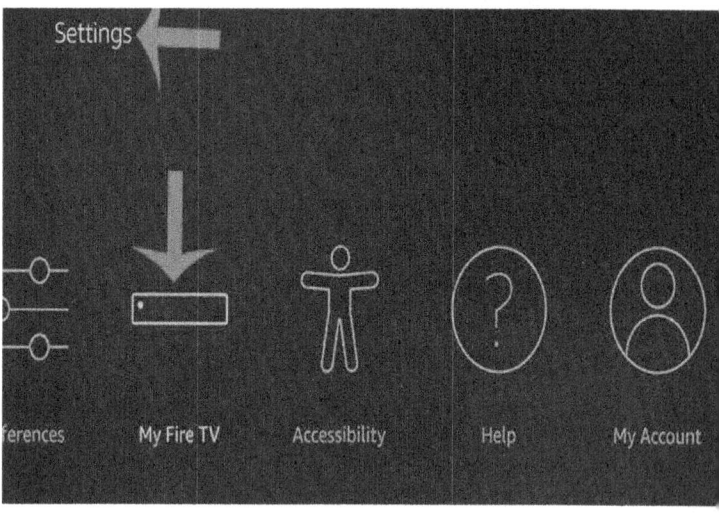

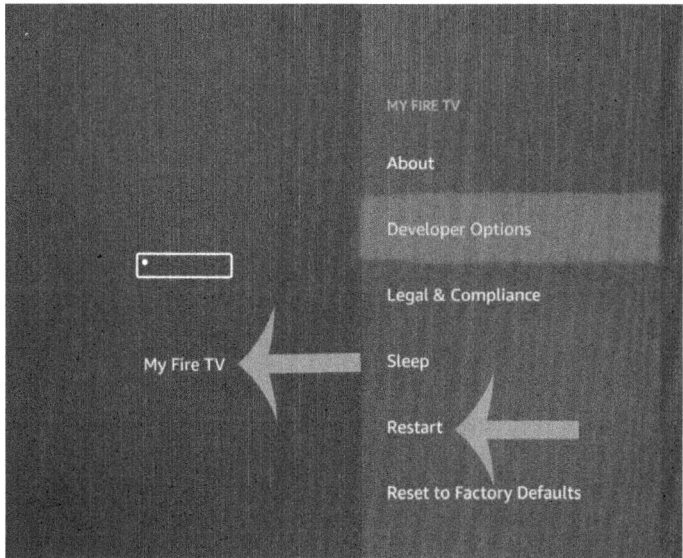

- Alternatively, you can unplug the adapter from the power supply to turn it off and then re-plug it to restart it.

How to Find 4k Content

Most users prefer to stream content in 4K, and this streaming stick allows you to do that. However, for this to work, you'll need an Ultra HD TV with at least one HDMI input that supports HDCP 2.2 content protection. HDPC (High Bandwidth Digital Copy Protection) is a digital content protection standard that makes ripping digital content extremely difficult. HDCP 2.2 is a new version that has been updated to protect 4K content specifically.

HDMI 2.0 is also required, which is only available on newer television models. Your Fire TV can instantly detect the HDCP 2.2 requirements, and the Fire TV Display Menu can show you whether your TV supports HDCP 2.2.

Furthermore, Ultra HD 4K streaming requires a high-speed internet connection of at least 15 Mbps. Netflix, for example, recommends a 20 Mbps internet connection for a better viewing experience. How to find 4K Content on Fire TV

- Head to your Fire TV's Settings, go to "Display and Sounds," and click on the Display option.
- Next, go to "Video Resolution" and select the Auto option to enable 4K mode.
- If you prefer to view content in 1080p mode, then select the option from here. However, once you start watching movies and series in 4K, streaming in 1080p may become impossible. That's it!
- If you have subscribed to any of these services, you can enjoy great 4K content on

Netflix, Amazon Instant Video, iTunes, VUDU, and other services.

How to Use Alexa

To begin, simply hold down the blue Alexa button and tell Alexa your request. With Alexa, you can easily search for your favorite content and control media playback,

If you own an Echo device, you can also use the Echo's microphones and smart speakers to control your Fire Stick, regardless of whether the remote is in your hand. This is a far better way to invest in Amazon's Alexa ecosystem.

How to Use the Alexa App

If you want better control and communication on your Fire TV, then download the Alexa app on your smartphone and introduce it to your Fire TV. With the Alexa app, you can connect your Alexa devices to your Wi-Fi network, provide Alexa with your location, connect to smart-home devices, provide the details of your Amazon account, and much more.

You can use the Alexa app to send voice requests to Alexa via your smartphone, which is a nice feature. That is precisely why the Alexa button was made. However, before using this feature, you must first allow Alexa to access your device's microphone. Here's how it works:

- Download the Alexa app on your smartphone, sign in, and then follow the onscreen instructions. Make sure you sign in to the Alexa app using the same Amazon account you use with the Fire TV device.

- Head to the Alexa app, tap on the Alexa icon and tap on Allow when prompted
- Tap on Allow in the location prompt to allow Alexa to use your location.
- Tap Done to save. You'll hear a tone alert if the setup was successful.

How to Connect Your Alexa Device to Fire TV

Your Alexa device can control your Fire TV. But first, you have to introduce both device, here's how:

- Head to the Alexa app, go to the Menu tab, click on Settings, and tap on "TV & Video."
- Tap on "Fire TV," tap on "Link Your Alexa Device," and then select your Fire TV device from the list.
- Tap Continue and select the Alexa device you want to use to control your Fire TV.
- If you have multiple Alexa devices, you can tap on each one to set them up.
- Tap on "Link Devices," and that's it!

Best Alexa Fire TV Commands

Watching content

"Alexa, open Hulu."

"Alexa, Pause/Play/Stop"

"Alexa-rewind"

"Alexa, forward 5 minutes"

"Alexa, skip 20 seconds"

"Alexa, next episode"

Finding content

"Alexa, show me nearby hotels"

"Alexa, show me Tom Cruise movies"

"Alexa, search for Vampires Dairies"

"Alexa, what's the weather?"

"Alexa, what's the forecast?"

"Alexa, what's the weather in New York?"

How to Use VPN on the Fire Stick/TV

This streaming stick transforms any TV with an HDMI connector into an Internet-connected streaming device with access to thousands of streaming content. Unfortunately, most streaming media content is geo-locked, meaning that it can only be accessible from certain regions.

That's where a Fire Stick Virtual Private Network (VPN) comes in handy. A VPN service hides your true location from the content provider, making it seem like you are in another country or region. That way, you'll be able to access content that is only available in the United States even if you aren't based there.

Which VPN Should I go for?

There are a lot of crappy VPNs out there, and using the wrong one will leave you frustrated. If you're not sure which VPN service to go for, these are the three best options:

1.   Surfshark

If you want a VPN that is both fast and reliable, Surfshark is the best option. In addition to its speed, Surfshark supports an unlimited number of devices and handles them all without lagging. That means you can install Surfshark on your Fire TV Stick without giving up one of the few connection options available.

2.   NordVPN- the VPN juggernaut

If you are a newbie to the VPN industry, NordVPN is your best bet. NordVPN boasts of good processing speed and promises a faster connection time following its next major update. Following its 2019 scare, Nord has gone 100 percent RAM-disk and now offers co-located and bare metal servers.

NordVPN has a large number of simultaneous connections, with six available on its network, compared to the five or fewer offered by practically all other providers. It also has a dedicated IP option for people who want a more secure VPN connection. NordVPN also offers a useful kill switch feature.

3. ExpressVPN

Since recovering from its server seizure issues, ExpressVPN has switched to 100% RAM-disk servers for even better privacy protection. ExpressVPN has a solid track record and includes a handy kill switch feature.

Unlike other VPNs, ExpressVPN accepts bitcoin as a payment method, which is a nice feature that adds another layer of security to the checkout process.

Yes, ExpressVPN is more expensive than Surfshark and most VPN services. However, the services it offers are well worth the money.

How to install a VPN from the Amazon app store

- Head to your TV's home screen, go to Apps, click on Categories, and then select Utility or run a search for "VPN."
- Select your preferred VPN from the list, e.g., NordVPN, and click on the yellow download button to download the app.
- Next, install the app, click on the yellow button next to Open to launch the app, and then log in using your username and password.

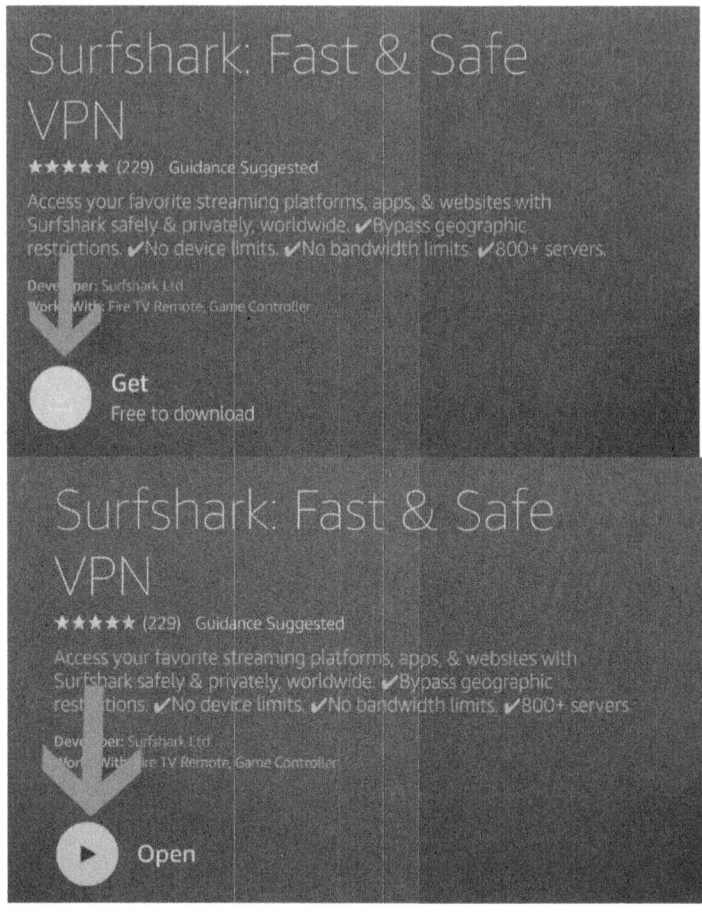

- Now click on the Connect button to connect right away, or choose your preferred location. That's it! You can now stream with the VPN running in the background.

Note: you won't receive any update notifications from the Amazon App Store if you side-loaded your VPN installation. Instead, you must first uninstall the VPN app before downloading the new native app.

If your preferred VPN app isn't available in the Amazon app store, here's how to get it via the Android app store.

- Download the VPN from the store and head to your Fire TV's Settings.
- Go to "My Fire TV," click on "Developer Options," search for the Downloader, and select Download.
- Click on Allow when prompted, click OK, and enter the URL of your APK installer.

- Click Go, then click on Install and sign in to your Fire TV. The app will activate after you sign in.
- Turn on the VPN and connect to your preferred server. That's it!

How to Use a Mouse with the Fire TV Stick

- Head back to the Downloader app, go to Settings, and click on "Enable JavaScript."
- Find your way to the Home tab and the APK URL "http://tinyurl.com/firetvmouse."
- Download and install the APK.
- Launch the app and then toggle on "Enable Mouse Service" in Settings.
- To turn the mouse on and off, quickly press the play/pause button on your remote twice.

How to update your VPN app

- Head to your Fire TV's home screen, click on the VPN app, and then click on "Menu and More Info" to open the app's detail page.
- Click on the Update button to get the latest software. The update button will be hidden if there is no software to update.

Troubleshooting

If you're having connection issues or your VPN PIN can't be validated, here are a few steps you can take to troubleshoot

- Clear the cache or data of the VPN app
- Restart your Fire TV
- Connect your Fire TV Stick to the new network with high signal strength.
- Uninstall and reinstall the app

- Switch protocols: head to Settings, and turn TCP off or switch to UDP.

CHAPTER TWO

How to Install Apps

The Fire Stick 4k max is the best streaming stick for Amazon users. This streaming stick offers a variety of movies, TV shows, games, and music. If you want to watch movies on Hulu or Netflix, go to the Amazon app store right now and download the app? Here's how to do that:

How to download apps from the Amazon app store

You can go through the countless apps in the Amazon app store and check what app is available for download. You can go to the Amazon App Store to check what's available for download. But first, make sure you have a secured internet connection.

- Head to the Fire TV's home screen, click on your remote's Up button, and then move through the menu until you get to the apps section.

- Press the "Down" button to open the apps tab, press your remote's Center button on an app to select it and then click on "Get" to install. Most apps in the app store are free. If it isn't, click on the small shopping cart icon to purchase it.

- When you're done, go back to the home screen to launch the app.

How to Use the Search Function to Find and Download Apps

You can use the search function to quickly locate an app in the app store. Here's how

- Head to the Fire TV's home screen and click on the small magnifying glass at the top left corner to open the "Search Function."
- Use your remote to type in the name of the app that you want to download.

AMAZON FIRE STICK 4K MAX GUIDE

- Select the app and click on "Get" to download it. If you're downloading the app for the second time, you'll see the "Download" button instead.

- Click on "Open" to launch the app.

If you are looking for a better way to launch the Search Function, you can also do that using your Alexa Voice Remote. To do that:

- Press the Alexa voice button on your remote and say the name of the app.
- Say "Get" when the app appears on the screen to download it.

How to Download Apps to a Fire TV Stick Using the Amazon Website?

There are different ways to download apps on your Fire Stick, and visiting the Amazon website is one of them. You can visit the Amazon website on your computer and install any app available in the store. Here's how to download apps using the Amazon website:

- Open your browser and go to amazon.com/appstore.
- Browse through the app's categories on the left-hand sidebar, locate your Fire TV Stick's model and check the box next to it.

> **New Releases**
> Last 30 days
> Last 90 days
> **Device Type**
> ‹ Clear
> ☑ **Fire TV** ←
> ☐ Fire Tablet
> ☐ Fire TV Edition TV
> ☐ Fire Phone
>
> **Fire Tablet Model**
> ☐ Fire HD 8 (10th Generation)
> ☐ Fire HD 10 (9th Generation)
> ☐ Fire 7 (9th Generation)
> ☐ Fire HD 8 (8th Generation)
> ☐ Fire HD 10 (7th Generation)
> ☐ Fire HD 8 (7th Generation)
> ☐ Fire 7 (7th Generation)
> ☐ Fire HD 8 (6th Generation)
> ☐ Fire HD 10

- Check the "Deliver to" box to open a new drop-down menu, locate your device on the list and click on "Get App" to download.

- Now head to your home screen to locate the newly downloaded app

How to Enable Third-Party Apps in Settings on Fire Stick

Despite the fact that the Amazon app store has several apps, there are still some that aren't available. Sideloading is the only way to get third-party apps on your Fire Stick. However, you must first enable third-party apps in Settings. Here's how it works:

- Head to your Fire TV's home screen, go to Settings, go to "My Fire TV," click on "Apps from Unknown Sources," and turn it on. That's it!

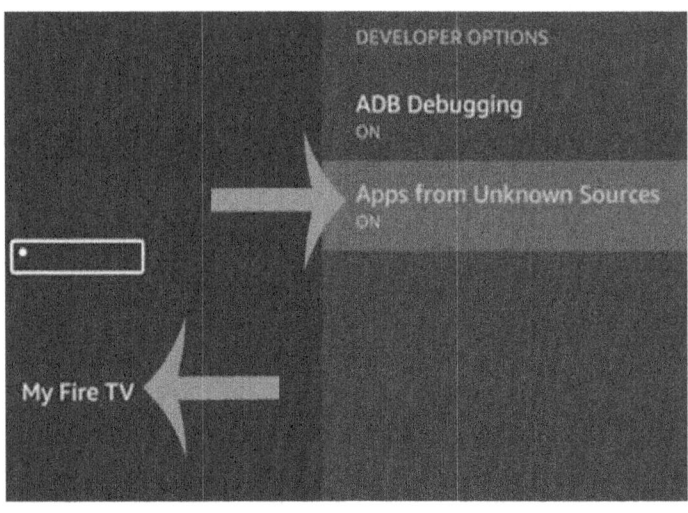

How to side-load apps

Method one

Amazon devices currently only support Android apps. The good news is that you can move them to your Fire TV device if you have them on your phone. Here's how to do it:

- First, connect your Fire Stick and smartphone to the same network
- Open the app on your phone and tap on the hamburger menu icon.
- Tap on "Select," tap on "Network," and allow the device to scan for available networks.
- To locate your Fire Stick, look for its device name and IP address and then click on it.
- Open the top bar section called "Local Apps," and locate the app you wish to install

- Click on the app and confirm to "Install." That's it!

- After installation, head to your Fire TV's home screen and locate the app.

Method two

The Downloader app from AFTVnews is another way to side-load apps. Here's how to use it:

- Firstly, install the app on your Fire TV and launch it. You can use the search function or your Alexa remote.

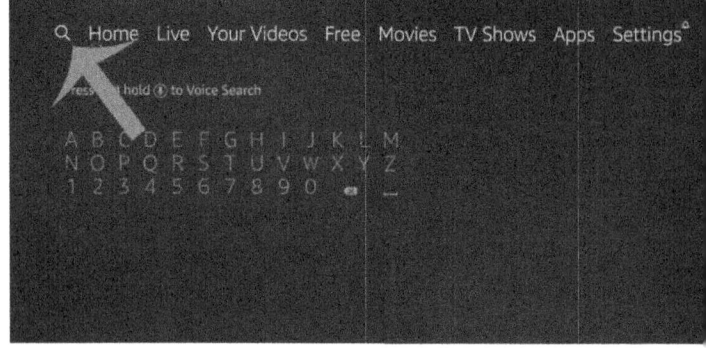

- Click on "Home" on the left-hand sidebar, click on "Enter URL," and then press the select button on your Fire Stick's remote control to open the keyboard.

- Type in the URL of the file you want to import and click on the "Go" button to start the download. Note that you'll have to save the file before doing this.

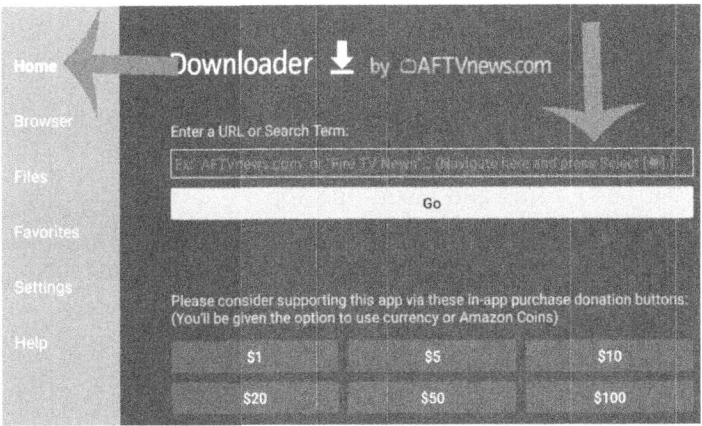

- Press the "Install" button after downloading the app to install it

- Click Open to launch your newly installed app. You can delete the APK file afterward.

You can also download files directly from the internet using Downloader's built-in browser. Here's how to do it:

- Open Downloader, click on "Browser," type in the address and click on "Go."
- Click on the hamburger menu icon and select "Fullscreen Mode."
- Scroll through the page, find the download link and install the app.
- Click Open to launch your newly installed app

How to Uninstall Apps

As you already know, this streaming device comes with many pre-installed apps that might take up a significant amount of your storage space. Deleting some apps will free-up space on your Fire Stick and help fix certain issues. I am going to show you three easy ways to do this. You can use these methods to delete both pre-installed apps and the apps you installed.

Method 1- App Settings

- Make sure your Fire Stick is connected to your device and turned on.

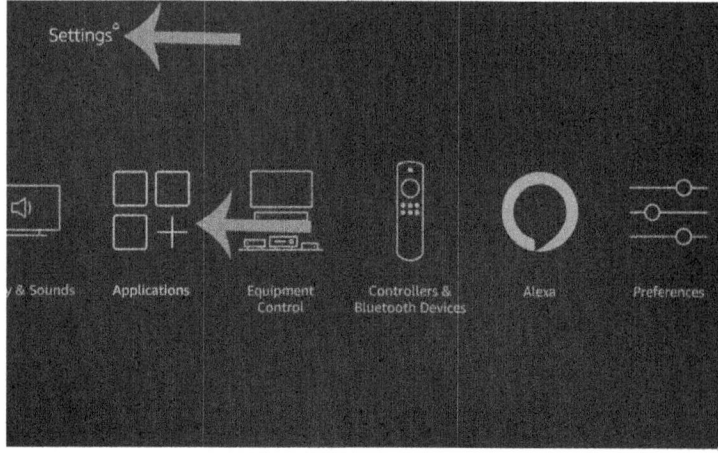

- Head to your Fire TV's home screen, go to Settings, go to Applications, and click on "Manage Installed Applications."

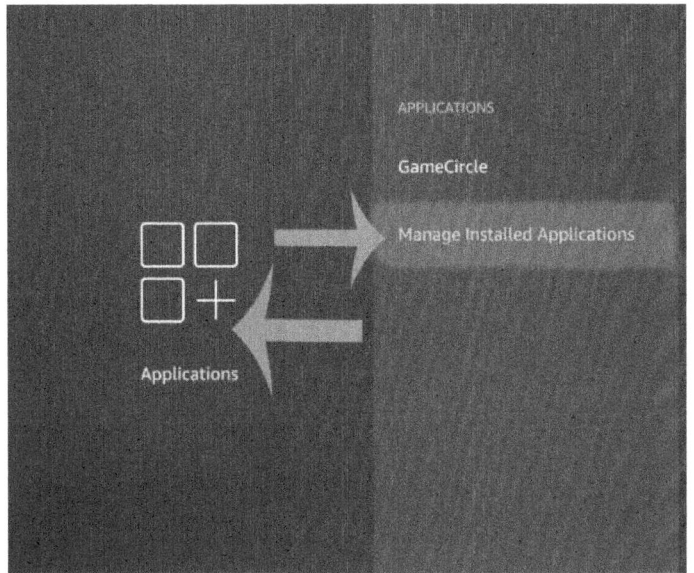

- Locate the app from the list, click on it, and click on "Uninstall."

- Click on "Uninstall" again when prompted to delete the app. That's it!

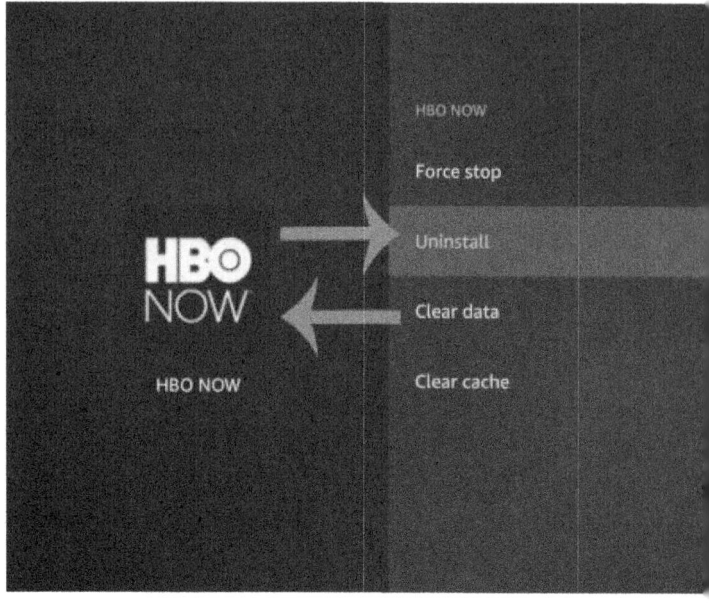

Method 2- Your Alexa Remote

- Make sure your Fire Stick device is connected and turned on.
- Press the home button, choose Apps, and press the Center button to select the app.
- Press "Uninstall" when prompted to delete the app.

Method 3- The ES File Explorer App

You can easily delete pre-installed apps on your Fire Stick with this file manager app.

- First, download and install the ES File Explorer on your Fire Stick.
- Launch the app, go to the Library section, and then go to Apps or press "App."
- Select the app from the list and click on "Uninstall" in the bottom menu.
- With this file explorer, you can easily delete multiple apps simultaneously. To do that, mark the checkbox for the apps you want to delete and click on Uninstall.
- Press OK to confirm. That's it!

How to Delete All Apps via Factory Reset

You may have noticed that the "Uninstall" option is hidden in some apps. This means that those apps are required for your Fire Stick to work smoothly. If you have several unimportant apps on your Fire Stick, you can perform a factory reset rather than delete them one by one. Here's how:

- Head to your Fire TV's Settings, go to "My Fire TV," and click on "Reset to Factory Defaults."
- Click on Reset when prompted, and that's it! This might take a while. So make sure you don't disrupt the process.

How to Clear an App's Data

If your Fire Stick has playback errors or you need to free up some space, you can clear an app's cache instead of uninstalling the app. Here's how:

- Head to your Fire TV's Settings, go to Applications, and click on "Manage Installed Applications."
- Select the app, and click on the "Clear Cache" option.

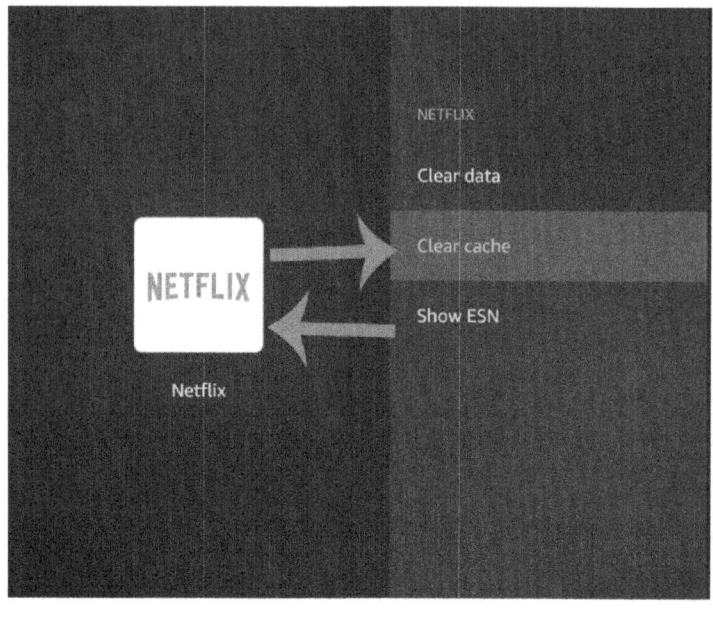

How to Update an App

You can enable automatic updates if you don't want to go through the stress of manually updating your apps. This action will upgrade your apps to their most recent version if you are connected to the internet. Here's how:

- Head to your Fire TV's Settings, go to Applications, click on "Appstore," and then turn on "Automatic Updates" from here.

If you prefer to update your apps manually, here's how to do that:

- Head to the Fire TV's Home Screen, go to Apps, open the app, and click on the "Update" button.
- The "Open" button will appear after the update has been completed.

How to Update Side-Loaded Apps?

There is no automatic update option for Side-loaded apps. So, you'll have to install an additional program and manually update them. Here's how:

- Head to the Fire TV's Settings, go to Device, click on "Developer Options," and ensure the "Apps from Unknown Sources" option is enabled.
- Now return to Settings, go to About and click on Network.
- Write down your Fire TV Stick's IP address.
- Go to the adbLink page on your computer, download the program and install it.
- Launch it, click on "New device," add your Fire Stick and insert the IP address.

- Install the newest version of the app you want to update on your Fire Stick.
- Open adbLink, and then click on "Install APK."
- Locate the.apk file in the adbLink interface on your browser. That's it! Your side-loaded app will be updated when next you turn on your TV.

How to Create an App Shortcut

Now you know how to install apps on your Fire Stick. However, some of your installed apps will not automatically appear on the home screen. That means you'll have to search for them on the internal menu. So, if it's an app you use every day, here's how to add it to the home screen:

- Head to your Fire TV's home screen and go to the "Apps and Games" section.
- If the app you are looking for isn't on this list, then hold down the Home button on your Alexa remote and click on the App option in the new menu.
- Here, you'll find a list of all your installed apps.

- Now search for the app you want to add to the home screen and click on your remote's Option button to open up a new menu screen.
- Click on the third option, which says "move to the front," to move the app to the home screen.
- Alternatively, you can press the Option button on your remote, click on the Move option, and then use your control to drag the app to the top of your screen.
- Now head back to the "Apps and Games" section, and you'll find the app sitting there. That's it!

How to use the Fire Stick Remote Shortcuts

Of course, you already know that this Fire Stick is a great streaming device. But what most users don't know is that this Fie Stick's Alexa remote has a lot of nice hidden key combinations to make navigation easier. Here are a few key shortcuts to save you a lot of time.

1. Adjust the Display Resolution

If you want to quickly change your display resolution, hold down the remote's UP Navigation + REWIND button to open the Resolution screen. From here, you can easily change your resolution settings.

2.   Reset your Fire Remote

If your Fire Stick is giving you issues, here is how to easily hard reset it; hold down the BACK + MENU + LEFT Navigation button for 15 seconds. This action will reset the remote, allowing you to pair it with another Fire Stick.

3. Reset your Fire Stick

Hold down the remote's BACK and RIGHT Navigation button simultaneously for ten seconds to reset your Fire Stick. That's it!

3. Restart the Fire Stick

To restart this device, hold down the SELECT and PLAY buttons simultaneously for 10 seconds

4. Open the System Menu

This is one of my favorite key shortcuts. To do that, long-press the remote's HOME button to open up the

Quick Settings menu. Here, you can access Mirroring option, Settings, and even Sleep settings.

How to Update My Fire Stick

By default, this streaming device should check for updates automatically every day. But if you want to check for updates manually, here's how to do that:

- Head to your Fire TV's Settings, go to the "My Fire TV," tab and click on About. On older Fire Sticks, the "My Fire TV" tab may still be labelled as "Device" or "System."

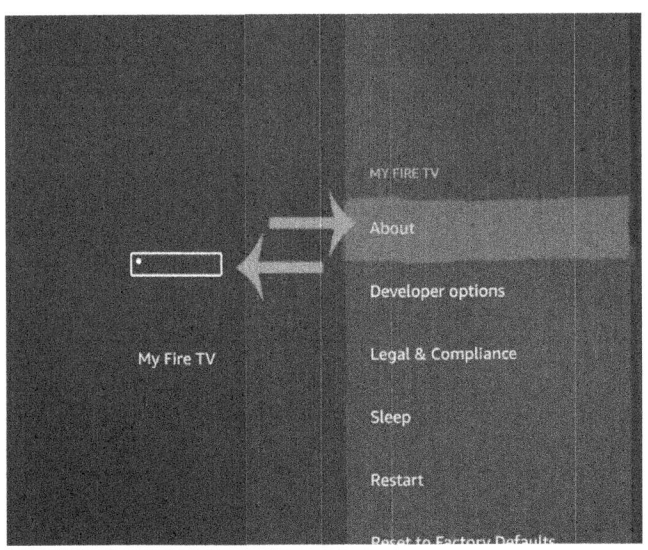

- Next, click on "Check for Updates" or "Install Update."
- You'll see the "Check for Update" option if the device is up to date.

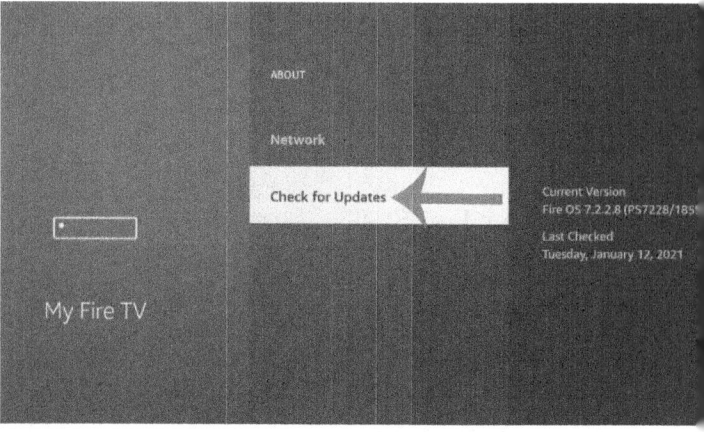

- If an update is available, you will see the "Install Update" option instead.

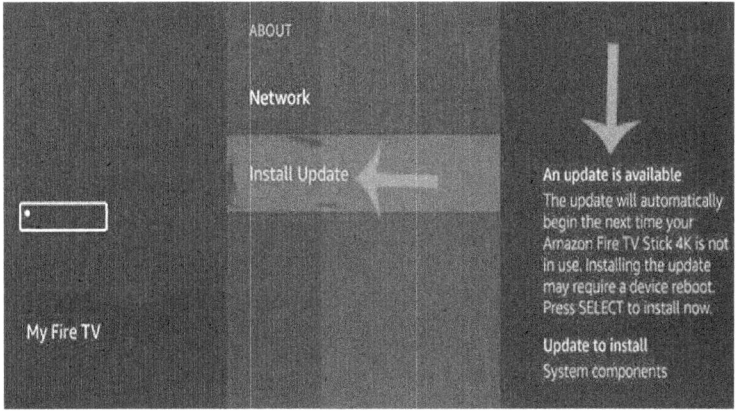

- Select the "Install Update" option and wait for the updates to be installed. Your TV will go off during the update process. So make sure you don't unplug the power cable.

How to Activate Sleep Mode

Sleep mode is a new feature on the Fire Stick that allows you to reduce energy consumption on your Fire Stick. So if you are energy conscious, this feature is a good one for you:

- Hold down the Alexa remote's Home button, go to Settings, and select the "My Fire TV" option.
- Now click on the Developer option, and click on "Deep Sleep" to put the Fire Stick to sleep. Note that network connectivity will be disabled in this mode.
- To wake it up, simply push the Select button on your remote. The Fire Stick might take a while to wake up.

Best Settings for the Fire Stick

If you want to enjoy your streaming experience, then changing your Fire Stick default settings is necessary. Note that you can always return to the default settings. So here's a list of the best settings for your Fire Stick:

1. Manage Your Privacy Settings and Disable Data Monitoring

Your Fire Stick 4k Max comes with a default data monitoring feature. This feature allows Amazon to monitor your data, which could compromise your privacy. To disable it;

- Head to the Fire TV's home screen, go to Settings, go to Preferences, and click on the "Privacy Settings" option.

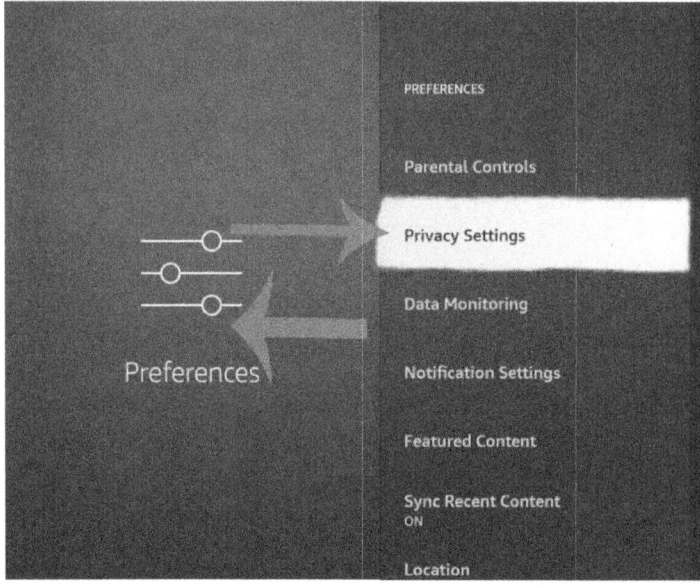

- Next, turn off the "Device Usage Data" and "Collect App Usage Data" options. Note that you can also disable interest-based ads on this screen.

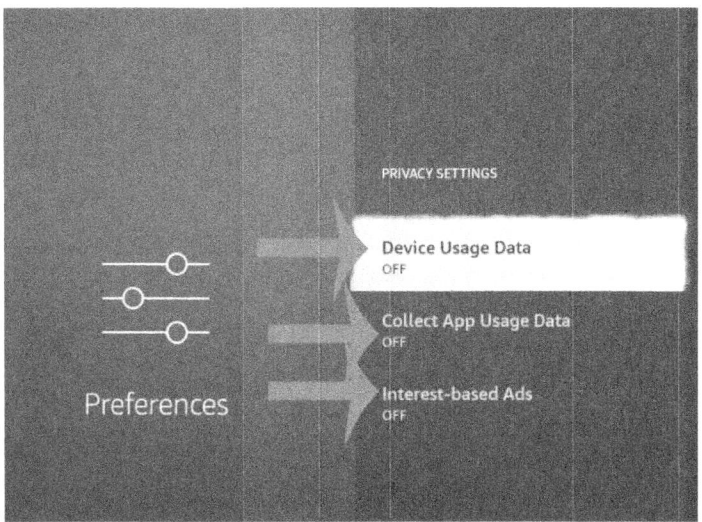

- Now head back to the Preferences menu, click on "Data Monitoring," and disable the "Data Monitoring" option on the next screen.

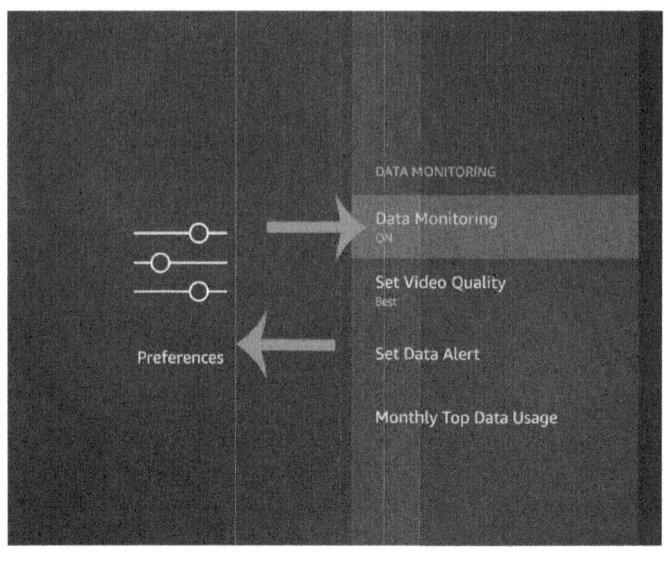

2. Change the Amazon App Store Settings.

There are a few settings in the Amazon app store that you can tweak to make your streaming time more enjoyable. Here is what you can do:

- Head to the Fire Stick's Settings menu, go to Applications and click on the "AppStore" option. Choose and then click the option Applications.

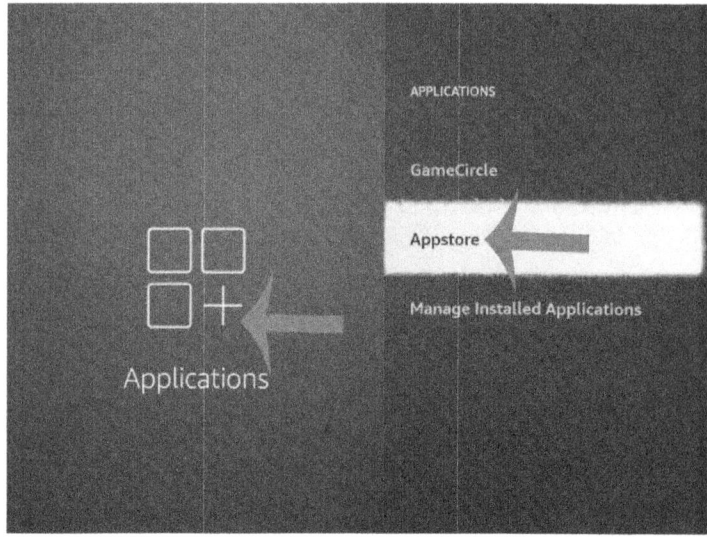

- Here, you'll find a list of settings you can change:

    o Automatic Updates: Enable this option so that apps will automatically update themselves whenever a new update is released. Note that this option works only with apps installed from the Amazon App Store.

- External Market Links: Certain apps feature links that take you to the Amazon App Store, where you can download other apps. Click this option and either choose "Ask Before Opening" (recommended) or "Don't Open."
- In-App Purchases: Disabling this option will help ensure that neither you nor your children make any in-app purchases by accident.
- Manage My Subscriptions: This option's only job is to take you to the Amazon site to manage your subscriptions.

- Notifications: Turn off this option if you don't want to receive notifications from the App Store

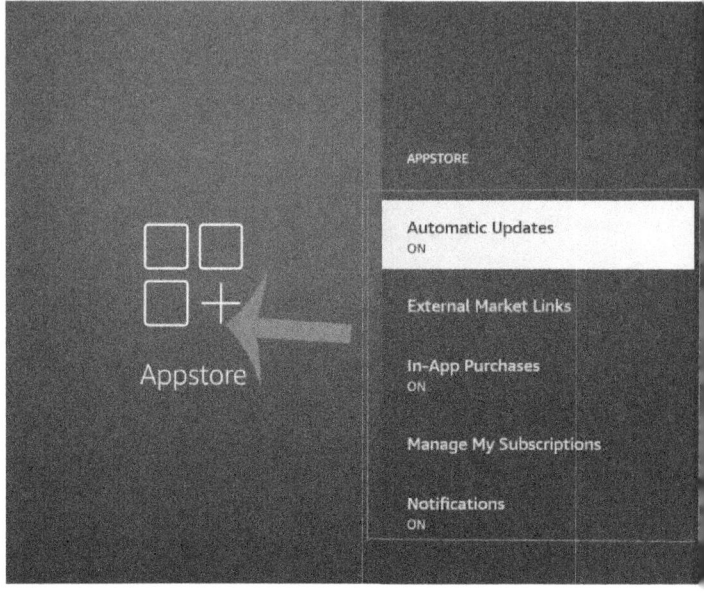

3. Change App Notification Settings

Having different apps popping up irrelevant notifications on your screen can be quite annoying. This will undoubtedly affect your streaming experience and get you a bit frustrated. Thankfully, you can choose to disable notifications for all your apps or just specific apps. Here's how to disable it:

- Head to the Fire Stick's Settings menu, go to Preferences, click on Notification Settings, and then turn on the "DO Not Interrupt" option to disable notifications for all your app.

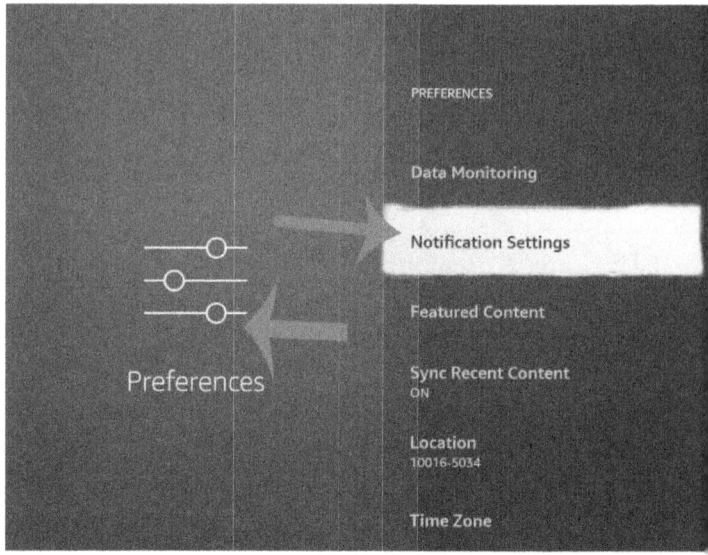

- Click on the "App Notifications" option and select the app from the list to disable notifications for specific apps.

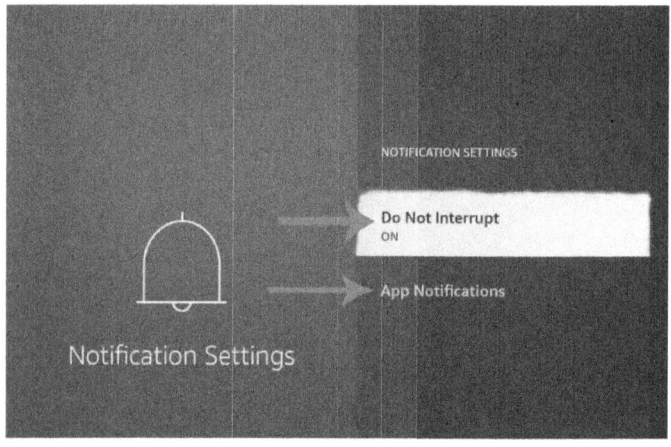

4. Disable Video and Audio AutoPlay

You can easily disable the AutoPlay feature on your Fire Stick if you find the feature annoying. If this feature is enabled and your home screen is left idle for even a few seconds, video, audio, and a preview of the content will automatically start playing. Here's how to disable this feature:

- Head to the Fire Stick's Settings menu, and go to Preferences.
- Next, click on "Featured Content," and then turn off the "Allow Video AutoPlay" and "Allow Audio AutoPlay" options.

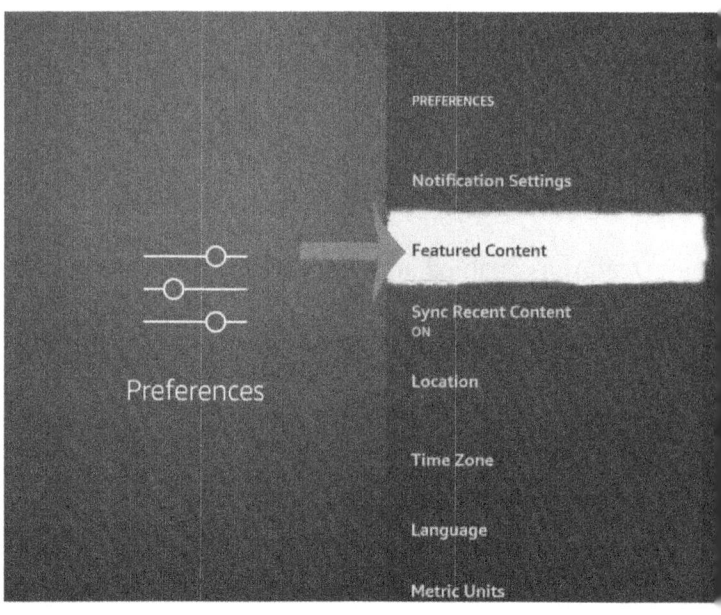

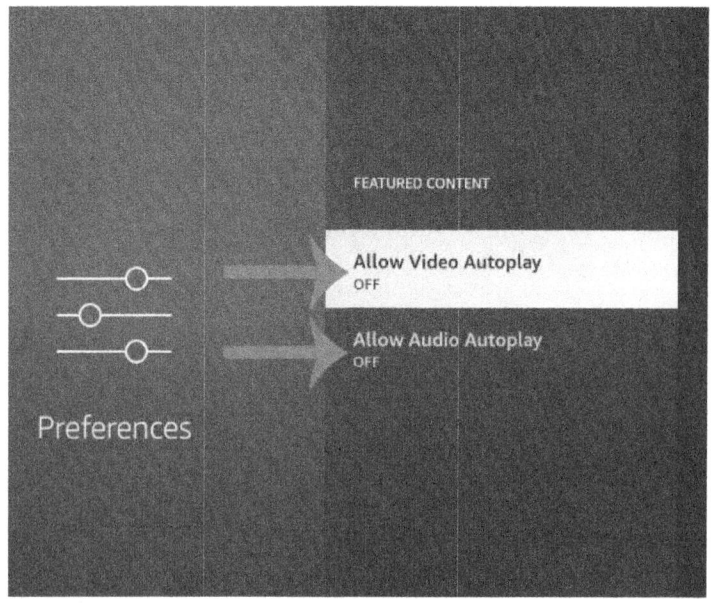

CHAPTER THREE

How to Manually Enable Parental Control

Amazon Fire Stick 4K includes a Parental Control feature that allows parents to easily restrict their children from accessing age-inappropriate content or from making unauthorized purchases. Let's take a look at how to set up both the PIN system, and parental controls

How to Manage Parental Control settings

This streaming stick has a lot of incredible apps and shows that may not be suitable for children. Fortunately, you can easily enable parental controls on the Fire Stick. But first, you need to head to your

Amazon action and activate a PIN in the parental control section. To do that;

- Sign in to your Amazon account, go to the "Account & Lists" tab, click on "Your Prime Video" and then click on the "Parental Controls" tab.
- Now use your Fire Stick to set up a 5-digit PIN. Note that you'll be needing this PIN later on, so save it somewhere.

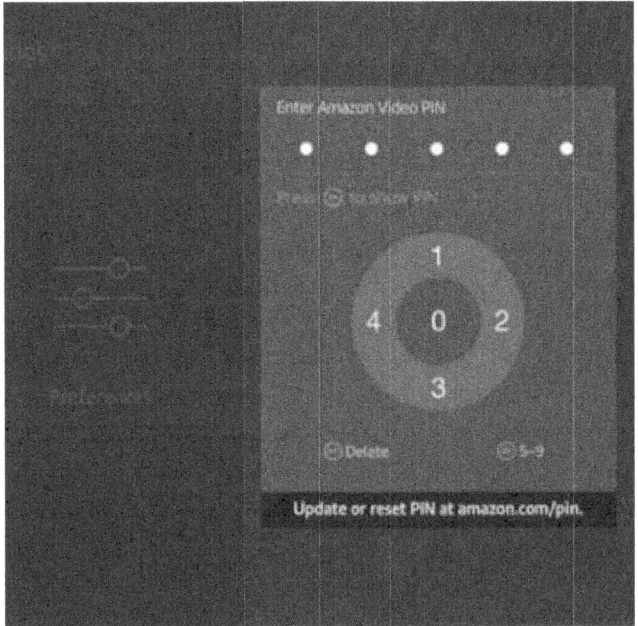

How to Enable Parental Controls

- First make sure the Fire Stick is plugged in.

- Once you've setup your PIN, head to the home screen, and go to Preferences,

- Next, click on "Parental Controls" from the list, click on the "Parental Controls OFF" option, and then enter your PIN when prompted.

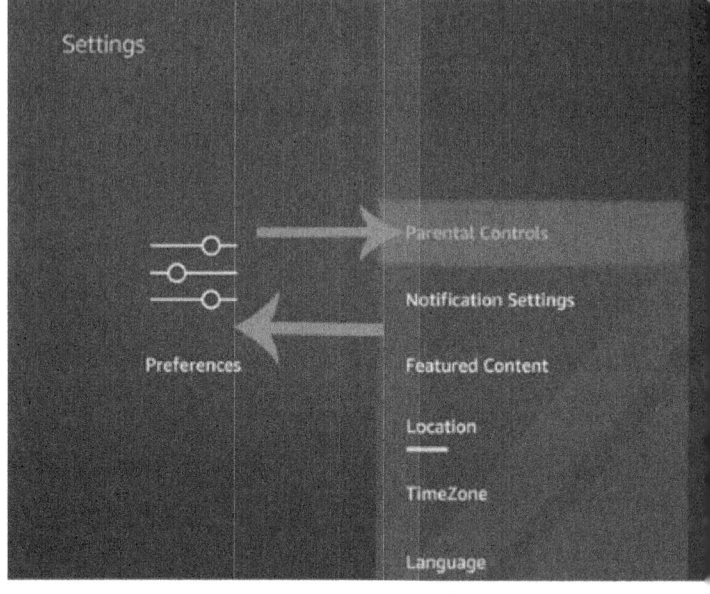

- Now click on OK to turn on the parental control feature.
- With this feature enabled, you'll be able to see other parental control options such as "Viewing Restrictions."

- If you choose to enable this restriction option, the viewing content will be restricted based on Amazon Video ratings of the shows and movies.

How to Change Parental Control PIN on Fire Stick?

- Head to the home screen, go to Preferences and click on "Parental Controls."
- Click on the "Change PIN" option to change your PIN

How to Disable Focused Adverts

You'll eventually see a lot of personalized adverts and suggested contents on your Fire TV, which can be annoying. If you prefer a clear content screen, then here's how to disable focused ads:

- Head to the Home Screen, go to settings, click on Preferences and then go to "Privacy Settings."
- Click on "Interest-based ads" and turn it off.
- Next, turn off the "Device Usage Data," and "Collect App Usage Data," options.

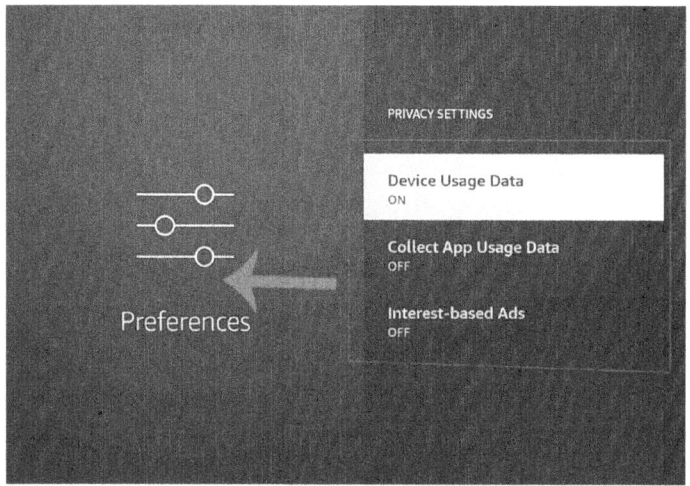

- Now return to the Preferences menu, click on the "Data Monitoring," option and turn it off.

- Return to the Preferences menu, click on "Featured Content," and turn off the AutoPlay options. That's it!

Adjusting these settings will block any focused ads from appearing on your screen.

How to Turn Subtitle On/Off?

With subtitles, aka Closed Captioning, you can read what is being said on a video. This is a nice feature for people with hearing impairment. Follow the steps below to enable/disable the subtitle feature. Note that these steps apply to the Fire TV as well as other smart TVs.

Main Fire TV Setting

- Head to the Home Screen, go to Setting, click on "Accessibility," and then click on the "Closed Caption" option.
- Press the "Center" button to toggle the subtitle feature on and off.
- If you enabled the subtitle feature, press the Down button to bring up other subtitle settings. You can press the Center button on

the new settings screen to change your options. That's it.

Amazon Prime Video

- Tap the Pause button and then the Menu button ≡ to access the settings menu
- Click on the Subtitles option and then use the Up and Down buttons to turn the subtitle option on/off.
- Press the "Play" button to resume the video

Netflix

- Press the Alexa remote's Pause button and click on the "Audio & Subtitles" options.
- While on the Subtitle screen, use the Up or Down button to select your preferred subtitle option.
- Press the "Play" button to quit the subtitle screen.

Disney+

- Press the Pause button, press the Up button and then select the Subtitles option.
- Use the Left and Right buttons to choose your preferred settings and press the Center button to select it.
- Press the "Play" button to resume the video.

YouTube

- Press the Pause button, go to the Captions option or click on the CC icon and then select your preferred subtitle settings.
- You can also access the "Caption style" settings and change your font style and size.
- Press the back button and then press the Play button to resume the video

Apple TV+

- Press the Down button to open the subtitle menu
- Choose your preferred language or click on the Off option to disable captions.

HBO Max

- Press the down button twice, and click on the CC icon
- Choose your preferred language or click on the Off option to disable captions

IMDB TV

- Press the Menu button ☰, go to Subtitles, and then turn off the subtitle option.

Sling TV

- Press the Center button, click on the "CC" icon, and then turn the subtitle option on/off

How to Use Netflix

Netflix provides a lot of interesting content to watch on your big TV screen. Netflix should be one of the first apps you install on your Fire Stick. Now, let's have a look at how to install and use Netflix.

- Head to the Fire TV's home screen, use the search field to locate the Netflix app, and click on the Download or Get option.
- After the download, launch the app and then sign up to start using the service.

How to Sign Up for Netflix

- Head to Netflix.com, enter your Email address, and click on "Get Started."
- Create a new password, choose your preferred subscription plan, and then choose your preferred payment method. Note that you'll

get 30 days' free trial period after verifying your payment method.

- Click on Finish to exit the Sign-Up page.
- Now head back to the Netflix app and sign in using your Netflix email and password. That's it

Note: If you live outside of the United States, you can still access all of the Netflix services available in the United States. Simply download a good VPN app to access these features.

How to Use YouTube

The YouTube app is available on the Amazon App Store and you can easily download it on your Fire Stick. Here's how to get YouTube working on this streaming device

Pro Tip: Use a VPN to access Netflix / YouTube to bypass online surveillance, ISP throttling, and geo-blocking content on.

- Head to the Fire TV's home screen, use the search field to locate the YouTube app and then click on Get or Download.
- After the download, launch the app and then sign up to start using the service.

How to Sign Up for YouTube

- Click on the Sign In option after launching the app
- Head to the website at- "youtube.com/activate" on your laptop or smartphone
- Enter the Sign In code and then sign in with your Google ID if you haven't done so.

Note that signing in to YouTube will unblock all the restricted content and let you see all your existing subscriptions, playlists, and history associated with your Google ID.

How to Use the Watch List?

A watch list, also known as My Stuff on Amazon Prime, allows you to keep a list of movies you want to view but don't have time to watch right away. If you've recently purchased this streaming stick, you're probably wondering how to access your watch list. Here is how to find a watch list on the Fire Stick:

- Head to your Home Screen, and click on the "My Stuff," tab to access your watch list. Your screen will be empty if you are a new user.

- If you are not a new user, you can easily remove an item by pressing the Menu button ≡ and clicking on the "Remove from List" option.

How to Add Content to The Watch List?

- Head to the Home Screen, go to Videos and then search the Prime Video Collection for a movie or TV show you want to watch.
- Press the Menu button ≡ on your preferred video and then click on the" Add to Watch list" option. That's it!

How to Use the X-Ray Feature?

The X-Ray feature in Amazon Prime allows you to see all the interesting information about each scene, character, and actor. You can now skip hundreds of steps of searching for information about a movie and get all that information at your fingertips using this feature. Here's how to use this feature:

- Head to the Fire TV's Home Screen, select your preferred movie and then click on the 'View All X-Ray' button at the bottom left corner. You can click on it to play/pause the video.
- Next, pause the movie and press the Up button on your Alexa remote to access the X-ray options list.

- Click on the "Scenes" options to skip through scenes. This is just like fast-forwarding the movie.
- Click on the "In Scene" option to get more information about the characters.
- Click on "Actors" to access information on the cast of the movie
- Click on "Characters" to see full details of the character in a particular scene. You can also select a character to see their bio and details.
- Click on the "Music" option to access your favorite piece of music in the film from the list of the soundtracks provided.

CHAPTER FOUR

How to Monitor Data Usage?

While watching movies on your Fire Stick is a fun way to unwind, it also consumes a lot of data. The perk of using this streaming stick is that you can always see and track how much data you're burning up. This feature is called Data Monitoring, which allows you to track your monthly data usage.

One cool thing about this feature is that it allows you to set your preferred data cap value. Once you've gone beyond the cap value, a notification will be sent to you, letting you know you've gone over the daily limit.

How to Check App Data Usage?

- Head to the Home Screen, go to Settings, click on Preferences, and click on the "Data Monitoring" option.
- Click "On" to enable the monitoring feature and access other options. You can also change your video quality once the feature is enabled.

Note that your data usage depends on your preferred video quality settings.

How to Set Data Cap Value?

- Click on "Set Data Alert" after the Video Quality option, and then set your preferred data cap value for each day. You'll be notified once you've hit the data limit.

Check App Data Usage by Apps

- Head to the "Data Monitoring" menu and click on the "Monthly Top Data Usage" option.
- Here, you'll find your data usage for each App. The Current Data Usage and Last Month's Usage are also displayed on the right tab.

With this feature, you can keep track of your monthly data usage and regulate it to avoid incurring additional charges from your Internet service provider.

How to Mirror Your Laptop to The Fire Stick?

The second screen feature allows you to connect a second device or screen to another primary device or T.V. You can use the Second Screen feature to watch content on your desktop or phone while the Fire Stick acts as the primary device.

Now, here's how to mirror your Fire T.V. screen on a windows 10 P.C:

First, you have to prepare your Fire Stick for mirroring. You can do this from your television, where the device is connected.

- Head to the Home screen, go to Settings, click on the "Mirroring" option, and then click "Enable Display Mirroring."

AMAZON FIRE STICK 4K MAX GUIDE

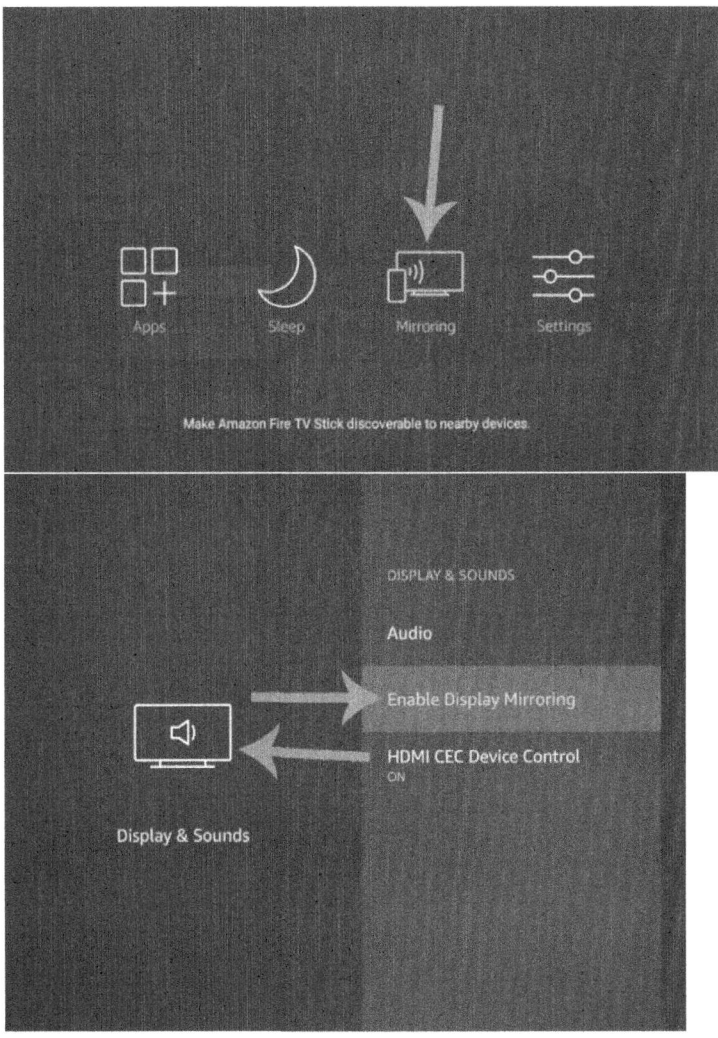

- Note that you may have to repeat this process if the setup isn't successful. Once you've set up the device for mirroring, it's time to focus on your computer.

- On your P.C., click on the notification icon at the bottom of the screen and then click on the Connect option. Or, you can use the key shortcut "Win+K" to quickly access the connection page directly.

- Now select your streaming device from the list. If the streaming stick doesn't appear on this list, then it means the mirroring setup wasn't successful. You may have to repeat the setup process.

- If the mirrored screen is too small, right-click on your desktop and then click on the "Display settings" option to change your resolution. Your second screen will work perfectly now.

In case you run into issues, make sure both devices are connected to the same Wi-Fi network and then reboot the Fire Stick.

How to Mirror Your Smartphone to The Fire Stick?

Amazon allows you to mirror your screen and enjoy your Fire Stick features on your smartphone. The setup process isn't techy or complex, so you don't have to worry. Here's how to go about it:

How to activate the Mirroring feature on your Fire TV?

Your Fire TV must first be set up for Mirroring activities before you can use any device as a second screen.

- Head to the Fire TV's home screen, go to Settings, click on the "Display & Sounds" option and then click on "Enable Display Mirroring."

Or, if you want to get this done quickly, you can:

- Hold down the Alexa remote's Home button to access the quick menu options and click on the Mirroring option. That's it! Your Fire Stick is good to go.
- This action will switch your Fire Stick into receptive mode, ready to receive input from any smartphone.

How to Cast an Android Phone

Mirroring your Android phone to this streaming stick is straightforward as most Android devices are integrated with Mirroring options. However, mirroring options defer from one Android device to another.

- Head to your smartphone Settings, use the search bar to locate the "Connected Devices" option, and click on it.

- Go to "Connection preferences," click on "Cast, Cast screen, "Wireless display," or on any other similar mirror display option you find.

- In the next "Cast" screen that appears, choose your Fire Stick from the menu and then click on the "Start now" option when prompted to launch the mirroring feature.

- Once enabled, your streaming stick will begin mirroring whatever is on your device's screen.

How to Cast iOS Phones and Tablets to your Fire Stick

Normally, the Amazon Fire Stick doesn't get along too well with iOS devices. So you'll need a third-party app called AirScreen to get this done. Here's how:

- First, install the AirScreen app on your Fire Stick, launch it, and then press Confirm when prompted. Note that you have to connect both devices to the same network
- Now use your iOS device to scan the QR Code on your TV screen.
- Next, choose your preferred mirroring screen size and follow the on-screen instructions to complete the process.
- Swipe down from the top of your iOS device to reveal your quick settings, and then click on

the "Screen Mirroring" option when you're done. That's it!

Mirroring via Third-Party Apps in Android

If you're experiencing trouble mirroring your Fire Stick to your Android device, then consider using a third-party app. On the other hand, most apps simply cast your pictures, recorded videos, and music. In other words, you won't always be able to mirror Netflix, Hulu, Amazon Prime, Google TV, and other streaming services.

The AllCast app is one of the most popular and reliable apps that supports several devices perfectly. The only downside of this app is that you may have to get the premium version to eliminate video length limits, ads, and splash screens.

- First, download the AllCast app on your streaming stick and Android device.
- Next, launch the app on both devices.

- On your Android, choose the content you want to mirror and then follow the instructions on your screen.

How to Use 5ghz Network on your streaming stick

Connecting to a 5ghz network is the best way to stream content online. This network ensures increased speed and performance. If you are a fan of streaming content or playing online games, this network's speed will come in handy. There will be fewer hitches and shorter buffering times in your videos due to this.

What Is 5GHz?

The strength of your router is measured in gigahertz (GHz). Routers are available at two different speeds: 2.4 GHz and 5 GHz. GHz stands for gigahertz per second, and 5GHZ is the faster of the two.

5GHz is a new addition to routers and ensures you download and stream content a whole lot faster.

Not all devices can currently handle the speed of this network, as most old devices aren't compatible with that speed on the router. This may be a problem with older televisions. Newer devices can operate on any network; however, 5GHz may perform better.

How to Switch Your Router to 5GHz

- Head to your computer's browser and type in the address- /192.168.1.1 into the address bar. If you use a Ubee router, type in this address instead- /192.168.0.1. Other brands may use different default addresses.

- You can quickly check your router's address by going to your Fire TV's settings menu, then to the Device section, and then to the About option. You'll find the router's address here

- Save the address somewhere and then type it into your browser'.

- Next, check your router for your password and username, and then use those details to log in. Contact your ISP if you can't find your login details.

- Once logged in, click on the "Change Wireless Settings" option and then switch to 5ghz
- Next, select your preferred channel. Channel 36 is the commonly used option.
- Save your changes and then restart your router. That's it! Your router is now on the 5ghz network.
- Now head to the Settings menu on the Fire Stick to see if the 5GHz network is available.

How to Pair Fire Stick with a Bluetooth Speaker?

As you already know, this streaming stick allows you to turn any regular TV into a smart TV. This streaming stick also has Bluetooth options to pair the Fire Stick 4k Max with any other Bluetooth device.

How do I connect the Fire Stick to Bluetooth devices?

- Turn on the Bluetooth device and make sure the device is in pairing mode.
- Head to your TV's Settings, go to Settings, click on the "Controller & Bluetooth Device" option, and then click on "Other Bluetooth Device."

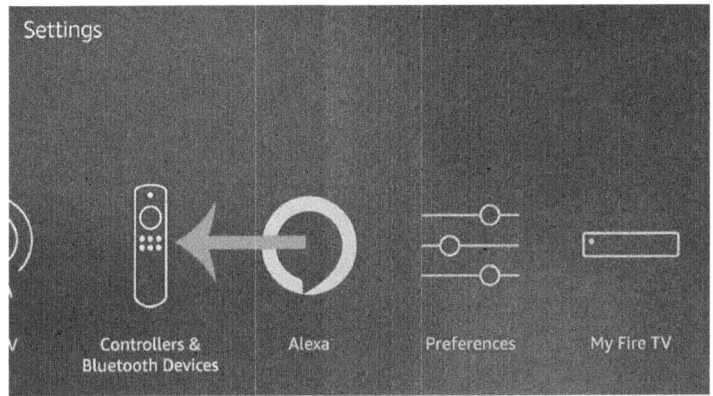

- Next, click on the "Add Bluetooth Device" and press OK when prompted.

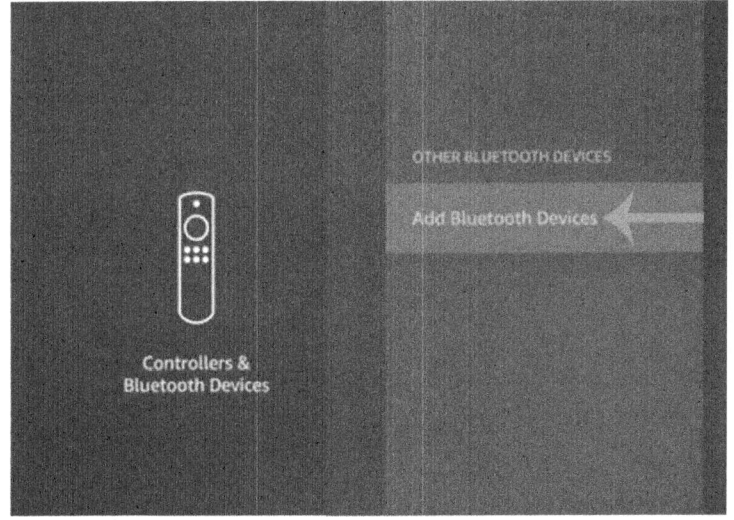

- Allow the Fire Stick to search for nearby devices and then pair the other Bluetooth device once the search is completed.

Always double-check that your Bluetooth device isn't connected to anything else. Note that you can also connect your headphones using the steps listed above.

If you are having any connection issues, you can:

- Turn the Bluetooth device off and on
- Read the device's manual on how to put it in pairing mode
- Disconnect the Bluetooth device from any other connected devices
- Use your TV's remote to increase the volume in case both devices are connected but you can't get any sound

- Plug the speaker into a power outlet to make sure it still has power

CHAPTER FIVE

How to Use Your Phone as a Remote?

If your Alexa remote is damaged or you can't seem to find it, there's no need to panic! Amazon allows you to use your smartphone (Android and iOS) to control and navigate your Fire Stick. Here's how to get it done:

How to Set up the Fire Stick Remote App

- First, download the app on your phone, launch it, and then sign in using your Amazon account email and password.
- Select the Fire TV Stick from the following menu, turn on your TV, and then switch the input associated with the streaming stick.

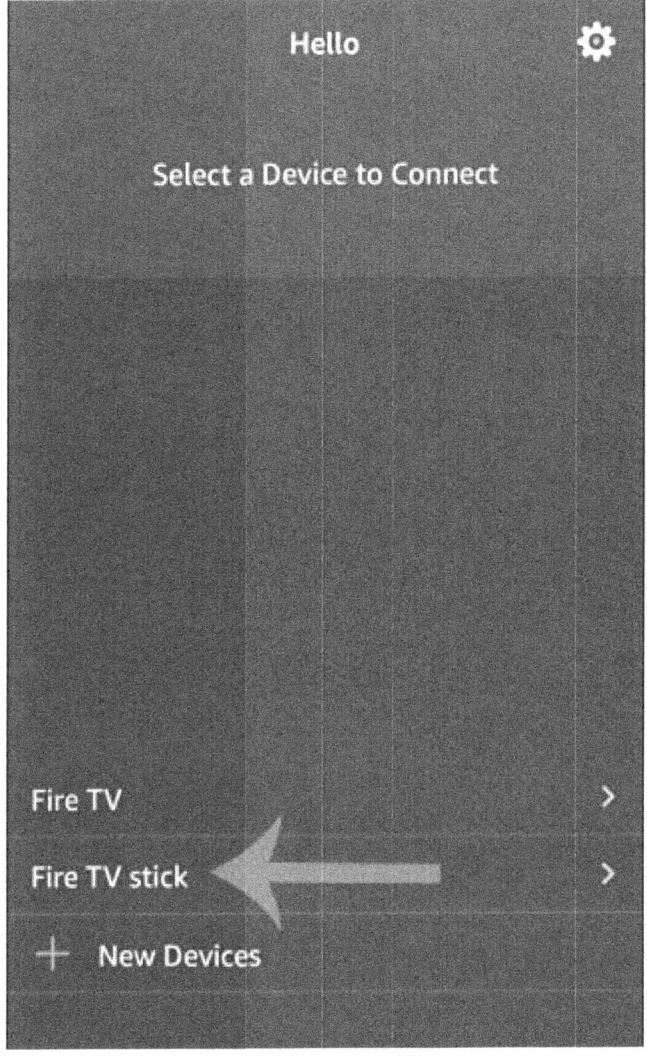

- Enter the request code on your TV screen in the app and then wait for the connection to be established. You can use the remote app to control your Fire Stick once the connection is successful.

How to Use the Fire TV Stick Remote App?

The phone app has the same buttons and functionality as your physical remote control. The differences between the physical remote and the remote app are:

- The touchpad is located in the middle instead of the usual circle button
- The remote app has a keyboard
- The app has a shortcut list that allows users to open any of their apps quickly.

Now, here's how to use the remote app:

- Tap anywhere on the touchpad area to select the currently highlighted item on your Fire TV

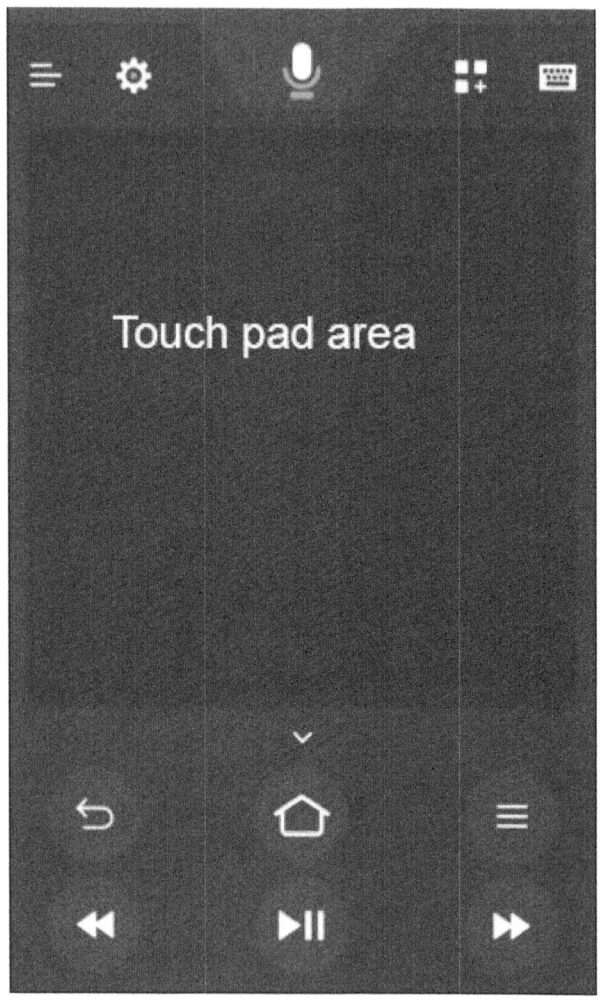

- Hold down on the touchpad area and then move your fingers left, right, up, or down to scroll in a specific direction.

- To move your selection without scrolling, swipe from the middle of the touchpad in the direction you want to move.
- Tap on the keyboard icon to access the keyboard menu
- To use the microphone, hold down on the mic icon and then speak to your phone. Note that voice controls are restricted to specific regions or countries.

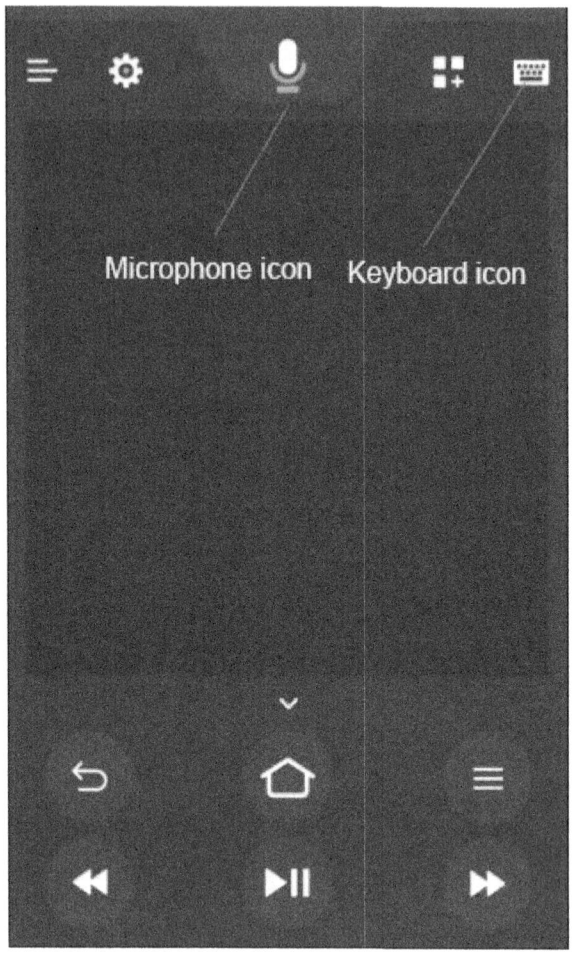

- Tap on the "Apps & Games" icon to access the Apps & Games shortcut menu. Tap on any app or game to launch it

- The return, home, menu, reverse, play/pause, and fast forward buttons all work the same way they do on the physical remote

How to Create a Digital Phone Frame On the Fire TV?

Creating a slide show of your favorite pictures and memories is one fun way to spark up old memories. Your Fire TV can do that for you in very simple steps. Here's how

Creating a Photo Screensaver

- Head to the Fire TV's home screen, go to the Apps menu, and click on the "Amazon Photos App" option.
- Select your preferred Photo or Photo Album. Here, you'll find all your favorite photos and albums.
- Select the images you want to use and then press the remote's menu button≡ once you are done to enter the screen saver menu.

- Once you select your preferred folder and photos, you can decide which photos will go after the other. You can also edit your slide time and the shuffle options.

How to customize photo slideshows?

- Head to your Fire TV's home screen, go to Settings, click on "Display and Sounds," and then click on the Screensaver option.

- Next, click on "Current Screensaver" and then change your album to whatever Amazon Photos album you prefer.

How to Configure the Volume and Power Controls?

The volume and power buttons on your Alexa remote don't always play nice with your Fire TV. Other buttons will function normally, but these two will appear to be off the hook. If you're having trouble getting these buttons to respond, try this:

- Head to the Fire TV's home screen, go to Settings, click on the "Equipment Control" option, and then click on "Manage Equipment."
- Click on the TV option and then click on Change TV
- Next, scroll through the list of TV brands, and select your TV brand

- Press the power button of your Fire TV remote on the next screen. If the button doesn't respond, press the No option to return to the first setup screen.

- Press the menu button≡ to access the Advanced Setup screen and then choose the IR profile of your TV when prompted. Note that there are over 12 IR profiles on the list, so identifying your TV's IR profile may take some time.

- If you don't know the IR profile, you just have to select each profile until the power button works.

- Once the power button works, use the same IR profile for the volume buttons.

- Save the remote setup when you are done, and then test the power and volume buttons to see if they work.

How to Install IMDB TV on Fire Stick

IMDb is a free-to-use streaming service owned by Amazon. Amazon Prime members can watch movies and TV series for free.

Usually, the IMDb app comes pre-installed on the Fire Stick. But if it isn't, here's how to add this app:

Method 1

- Head to your TV's home screen and use the search icon at the top to go to the Amazon App Store.

- Type IMDb TV in the search bar and then click on the search result when it appears on your screen.

- Next, click on the Get or Download options to install the app

- Once installed, launch the app and sign in using your Amazon Prime account. That's it!

Method 2

- Open your phone or computer browser and type in the URL http://amazon.com in the address bar.

- Log in using the same Amazon details on your Fire Stick, and then use the search field to locate the IMDb app easily.

- Click on the search result when it appears on your screen and then click on the Get or Download options to install the app

- Once installed, launch the app on the Fire Stick and then log in using your Amazon Prime account details.

CHAPTER SIX

Troubleshooting Issues

Can't connect to a Wi-Fi network

If your Fire Stick can't seem to load any content, first check to see if the streaming stick is connected.

- Head to the TV's home screen, click on Settings, and go to network. If you can't connect to your network, double-check that you're entering the correct password.

- If you can't find your Wi-Fi network at all, then check to see if other devices are having the same issue. If not, make sure that both devices are in range, and then try to reboot your modem or router to solve the problem.

Fire TV logo is stuck on the screen

If you turn on this streaming device and you can't seem to get past the logo screen, then try unplugging the Fire Stick from the TV and its power source.

If the streaming stick remains stuck, make sure the Fire TV is receiving enough power from the power source. Give the device 25 minutes to load, and then try a different HDMI port on your TV if the issue persists.

Fire Stick won't turn on

If your Fire Stick doesn't power on, try changing your batteries first. Unplug the Fire Stick, plug it back in, and force-reboot the device. Lastly, double-check to see if the Fire Stick's power source is plugged in properly.

Apps crash or refuse to load

The first thing to try out when any app refuses to load or continues to crash is to clear the app's cache Here's how to do that:

- Head to your TV's home screen, go to Settings, click on Applications, and then click on "Manage Installed Applications."
- Next, select the app from the list and click on "Clear Cache and Clear Data."
- If this action doesn't solve the issue, try to uninstall and reinstall the app.

Fix Screen Mirroring Issues

If you're having mirroring issues, first check to see if both devices support this feature. The Fire Stick doesn't support screen mirroring on iOS devices and Mac computers. To check if your Fire Stick supports this feature;

- Hold down the Alexa remote's Home button. If you see the Mirroring option, it means your Fire Stick supports this feature.

Update Your Fire Stick

Update your streaming stick is the best way to fix bugs and improve your streaming experience. If you haven't received software updates for a long time, here's how to get it done:

- Head to your TV home screen, go to Settings, and then to the "My Fire TV" option.
- Next, click on About and click on the "Install Update" option. If any updates are available, the device will automatically start the download.

Made in the USA
Coppell, TX
27 April 2023